IGNITE
FLAME
WITHIN

Guide to Healing

MYA SOUL

Igniting the Flame Within
Copyright © 2022 by Mya Soul

Tellwell Talent
www.tellwell.ca

ISBN
978-0-2288-7315-0 (Paperback)
978-0-2288-7316-7 (eBook)

Dedication

I would like to start by thanking Daphne Rose Johnson, who was the original founder of the brand name *Igniting the Flame Within*. We met under unusual circumstances, but the universe never ceases to amaze me.

Secondly, I would like to acknowledge you, the reader. I am so proud I of you! *By igniting the flame within me, I am now able to ignite the flame within you!* I feel honoured to be a part of your journey as you are now part of mine. I wish you all the best!

Disclaimer

The techniques, processes, ideas and suggestions in this book are not intended as a substitute for the medical recommendations of physicians or other healthcare providers. Use of the techniques in this book are at the reader's sole discretion and risk. The author takes on no responsibility for any negative consequences for following exercises provided within this book.

Igniting the Flame Within is spiritually-based learning with respect to all religions and all personal beliefs as we are all one.

Table of Contents

Introduction

For those of you who have not read my first book, Igniting the Flame Within, My Twin Flame Story to Union, Here's a quick recap . . .

August 24ᵗʰ, 2019 is a day I will never forget. I hosted a school reunion. At the end of the night, I went to hug everyone goodbye. That was the exact moment my life was forever changed on a soul level.

As I went to hug the last person goodbye, I felt the energy surge between us. A fireball of energy ignited within my root chakra, and within seconds, this fireball of energy burned through each charka and shot out the top of my head like a firework. I now know that what I experienced was called a kundalini spiritual awakening. *(At the time this happened, I didn't even know what a chakra was never mind the kundalini).*

When he walked away, I thought, *WOW! What was that? Where are you going? Why are you leaving me here? Take me home with you, I LOVE YOU!*

These were all weird thoughts to have considering I was at home, and I was married to someone else.

As he drove away, I felt as if my heart had been ripped from my chest and stabbed to death. I had never felt heartache and pain that excruciatingly bad before. This was all weird since I had not seen or spoken to this person in over twenty years. I had thought of him periodically over the years we were apart. I didn't think too much about it as he was my first childhood crush, and you never forget your first crush. What I felt was more than just a little crush you might have on someone. What was happening between us was indescribable.

Over time, I realized that I had become full-blown telepathic with him. He was obsessively in my headspace 24/7 (it was very annoying). I didn't know what was happening, why it was happening, how it was happening, or how to make it stop. I started to see visions through his eyes. He was sending me sexual energy from a distance.

The rose-coloured glasses came off instantly. I saw my husband for who he really was. I couldn't stand to be around him; his energy alone was so toxic that it made me physically sick. Not to mention I came to the realization that he was abusing me on so many levels.

To top it off, I was seeing shadow people and orbs. I was receiving spirit messages and downloads at an alarming rate.

I thought I was going insane. I tried to explain this to close friends and family, but no one understood it because they weren't experiencing it. I realized three weeks after we made this connection that he was something called a "twin flame."

I thought I was married to my soulmate. I was not looking for a twin flame; I didn't even know what a twin flame was. I started to research what I was experiencing to find answers as to what was happening to me. There were a lot of books on how to attract your twin flame into your life. Many of these books were written by people who thought they were on the twin flame journey. It turned out that they were using the twin flame label but explaining a soulmate connection. I go more in-depth about soul connections in my first book.

Soon after discovering that I was on the twin flame journey, I started to look for "specialists" to help manage the connection. I was anxious to learn how to quickly heal myself so my twin flame would come back. I spent thousands of dollars trying to "fix" the connection and ended up scammed, with little to no result for my money.

I was told by so many different "healing professionals" to forget about the twin flame label. Forgetting about the connection was much easier said than done. He was in my head 24/7. I didn't know how to turn it off. I was told that I needed to love myself first. Only then would he come back. So, I thought that once I did this "work" that I was "supposed" to do, we would live happily ever after. Nothing seemed to be helping and he wasn't coming back. I was trying all these different "therapies" and hired all these different "professionals" to help me. This was making things worse not better. I had all this random advice and nothing made sense anymore. I didn't know what to do or how to fix it.

The problem was that I was looking outside of myself for the answers. This was a journey of the soul. Before I came back into the physical world, my soul had signed up for this contract to have this experience so I could share my experience with others. I was chosen to be a leader. All the answers I was looking for were within me the entire time.

I realized along the way that the purpose of the twin flame journey was not so much about being with the other person romantically. Twin flames are not so much romantic partners but the path back to finding yourself. I needed to feel this intense connection in order to make the necessary changes to live my best life. This is not to say that a twin flame couple can't come together in a healthy relationship once the energy is balanced. I needed to learn how to take the focus off him and heal myself on a soul level. There was only one problem. *How?* Which brings me to where I am today!

Who Am I?

I am a warrior, a woman who knows her worth!
I am part Water, I flow in and out of people's lives
I am part Earth, I support universal growth
I am part Air, I am always there, just breathe
I am part Fire, I ignite the flame within
I am whole, a leader, healer and a guiding light

CHAPTER ONE

30 Day Self-Love and Care Challenge

I created the 30 Day Self-Love and Care Challenge to help with my own lack of self-love and care. The items I used to complete this challenge are linked to the blog on my website (www.myasoul1111.com). It takes three weeks to create a healthy habit. After three months, it becomes a sustainable healthy lifestyle change. Complete one task a day for 30 days. Some tasks are to be completed daily. Go at your own pace and do what feels right for you. I encourage you to step outside your comfort zone and try something new. However, if something doesn't feel right or isn't working for your lifestyle, switch it for something that fuels your soul.

1) Journal
2) Exercise
3) Drink more water
4) Meal prep and eat healthy
5) Write down ten things you're grateful for
6) I am . . . Daily affirmations
7) Ground yourself
8) Meditation
9) Take a bath with Epsom salt, bubbles, essential oils or bath bombs
10) Do something you love
11) Save $5 a day starting today until the end of the challenge
12) No screen time (and limit screen time moving forward)
13) Go for a walk or hike and connect with nature
14) Oil pulling
15) Forgive your past and let it go
16) Pay it forward
17) Take a different route to all your destinations today
18) Talk to a stranger
19) Compliment everyone you see
20) Declutter and get rid of things you no longer use

21) **Dance and sing throughout the day**
22) **Go to bed early**
23) **Try a new exercise**
24) **Make a meal you have never made before**
25) **Write down ten things to manifest into your life**
26) **Do something nice for a family member or friend**
27) **Get dressed up and go out for dinner**
28) **Do something out of your comfort zone**
29) **Call a friend or family member on the phone**
30) **Congratulations! You have completed 30 days! Treat yourself to a reward, you deserve it!**

Journal

I wrote my daily thoughts into a notebook. Which in turn I published into a tell-all book. There are many different types of journals that you can purchase. There are self-love workbooks and burn journals that help guide you through what to write. I also have two different dream journals. One where I write down my dreams as they come to me at night, and a second where I write down my hopes and dreams that I manifest into reality. In addition to journaling, I enjoy painting, doodling, drawing and colouring. Pick a journaling technique that works best for you.

Exercise

I have an educational background in recreation and leisure as well as overall wellness, fitness, and nutrition. I exercise for at least an hour a day. I switch up my routine regularly. The Canadian recommendation for an adult over the age of eighteen is a minimum of 150 minutes of vigorous activity per week. Exercises can be done ten to fifteen minutes at a time if you don't want to do it all at once. Ideally, you should exercise three to four times a week. I normally switch up my routine every four to six weeks. Schedule exercise into your daily routine as if it is an important appointment. It can be something as simple as adding a fifteen to twenty-minute brisk walk to your daily routine.

Drink more water

I start every morning with at least two cups of water upon waking. I like adding electrolytes to my water to keep hydrated longer and it adds flavour. You can buy electrolyte powder at the grocery store, pharmacy, health food stores and on Amazon. I enjoy warm lemon water in the morning, which is warm water with lemon, turmeric root, ginger root, 1 tsp honey, and a little cayenne or black pepper to activate it. This mixture helps boost the metabolism. It also works if you're starting to get a cough or sore throat. Of course, plain water is always the best option. To figure out how much water you should drink a day, there are daily water intake calculators online.

Meal prep and eat healthy

We all know how to eat healthy, but taking the time to meal prep is what takes the most work. When I experienced the kundalini awakening, I could no longer eat a lot of foods which I thought were healthy for me. I discovered that I'm allergic to eggs. I used to eat an omelet every day for breakfast. My body finds it challenging to digest proteins, meat, dairy, eggs and wheat. I had additional testing done, and I discovered that I have many food sensitivities and allergies. By eating these foods, I was keeping my body inflamed. With the help of a naturopath and holistic dietitian, I was able to make some minor changes to my diet. I have sustained a healthy diet that provides me with all the nutrients my body requires. Today, I am almost vegan. It helps that I had taken courses in food and nutrition prior to the awakening.

Start by trying a food elimination diet or the FODMAP diet. These diets are not for long-term use. You can follow them for two to six weeks at a time as a reset. Then slowly reintroduce food items back one at a time on a weekly basis until all food is back into your diet. I try not to eat any processed food and make everything from scratch. I add vitamins C, D, a multi-vitamin, probiotic, iron and fish oil. I completed a parasite cleanse while I reset my diet. I came to the realization that I also had parasites, which opened a whole other can of worms, so to speak. I now do a parasite cleanse once a year to restore my gut health. I increased my fiber intake by using G.I Fortify powder or Psyllium husk powder.

Warning! When doing a food elimination diet and detoxing the body, it's normal to feel sick, dizzy, nauseous, and experience headaches and body shakes. Detoxing from refined sugar can be comparable to detoxing from a drug.

A list of common food sensitives:

Dairy	*Chocolate*
Eggs	*Citrus Fruits*
Wheat/Gluten	*Coffee*
Soy	*Sugar*
Nuts	

The two most common food groups that were stopping me from reaching my goals were . . . dairy and wheat/gluten!

Dairy

Sources: milk, cheese, butter, eggs, yogurt, cream, ice cream. I learned how to substitute dairy with almond milk or coconut milk. If baking, I use avocado instead of butter. Flaxseed or chia seed grounded up with water makes an egg-like paste and helps as a binding agent while baking.

As an example, one of my favourite treats to make is chocolate avocado pudding.

Chocolate Avocado Pudding

- 1 avocado
- 1 tsp vanilla extract
- 1 can of coconut milk
- 1 tbsp cacao powder
- 1 tbsp honey

Blend and pour into a shallow dish. Refrigerate, or you can freeze them into popsicle molds for a treat.

<u>Wheat or Gluten</u>

I make all my food from scratch and no longer eat bread. I use almond meal or brown rice flour instead of regular flour when baking. I also make black bean brownies and chickpea cookies. These recipes can be found online.

I had to change the way I ate for health reasons. Navigate your own healthy eating journey. Eat foods that fuel your body and make you feel good. Don't treat it as a diet, think of it more as a sustainable lifestyle change.

Igniting the Flame Within

Helpful tip: if you're on a food binge, chew gum or brush your teeth!

Write down ten things that you're grateful for

Every day, I write down a minimum of ten things that I am grateful for. It can be something as small as the sun is shining. It's important to be grateful for the little things in life. This will attract more positivity. Which in turn helps raise your energetic vibration.

I am . . . Daily affirmations

I write affirmations on post-it notes and post them all over my mirror in my bedroom.

9

A few examples of what I write

I am beautiful	*I am blessed*
I am powerful	*I am courageous*
I am smart	*I am in control of my life*
I am loved	*I am a survivor*
I am abundant	*I am a leader*
I am a free spirit	*I am confident*
I am brave	*I am sunshine*
I am fearless	*I am a warrior*
I am unstoppable	*I am creative*
I am wealthy	*I am awesome*
I am worthy	*I am the creator of my life*
I am positive	*I am brave*
I am whole	*I am gorgeous*
I am capable	*I am healthy*
I am amazing	*I am strong*
I am proud of me	*I am trusting*
I am independent	*I am a Goddess*
I am successful	*I love myself*
I am caring	*I accept myself just the way I am*

When I first started the affirmations, I would just read them and didn't truly believe what they said. It was once I felt the energy shift that I started believing what

I had written. That was when my perspective changed. I realized that I am all of those things. I just needed to feel it within, on a soul level. I can now stand naked in front of the mirror. I love and accept myself exactly the way I am. Whereas before I would run past a mirror naked and try to get dressed as quickly as possible. I always saw the last ten pounds that needed to come off or an extra roll or wrinkle. I now see myself for the beautiful soul I am. *I am all of these things!*

Ground yourself

There are many different ways and techniques you can use to ground yourself. I personally like to ground myself while in the shower. I close my eyes and visualize the water running over my body like the energy flowing through my body. As the water is running down, I visualize all the dark, black, negative, toxic oozing energy going down the drain. I visualize my feet growing roots, and the roots crashing through the floor, all the way to the core of the earth. The roots wrap around the center of the earth, grounding me. I visualize the black ooze turning into liquid gold as it pours out of my body, nurturing Mother Earth. I release the negative energy with love and light. I visualize the sunshine, gold and pure white light circling my entire body until I feel that this process is complete. Other suggestions for grounding yourself are:

- *Walk on the grass barefoot*
- *Hug a tree*
- *Eat dark chocolate*
- *Run your hand under cold water and splash it on your face*

Meditation

When I first tried meditation, I thought I needed to sit cross-legged on the floor in silence. Turn off my brain and think about nothing. I mean, you can try that. I don't know about you, but I have constant thoughts in my head. There are lots of self-guided meditations and music that you can listen to on the internet. I find it easier to lay down to meditate, or I go for a walk in nature. I concentrate on my breath. In through my nose, out through my mouth—slow, deep breaths. I meditate when I first wake up, before bed, while out in nature, or in the bath/shower. There is no right or wrong way.

I get a lot of spiritual downloads during mediation. I personally try to focus on how I feel in that moment. If I'm outside, I focus on the warm sunshine on my face, the wind in my hair, the sounds of the birds chirping. I let the visions flow in naturally; I don't force anything. I don't worry about what tasks need to get done; I stay grounded and present. I use meditation paired with visualization techniques to protect my energy, and to connect with my guides and higher self. First thing in the morning, I put on a protective coat of armour through visualization. This armour protects me from negative energy that I may encounter throughout my day. This is protection from those who I call energy vampires and soul suckers.

Note: It's important to ground yourself before you meditate.

Take a bath with Epsom salt, bubbles, essential oils, or bath bombs

For best results, use two cups of Epsom salt. I enjoy dry skin brushing before having a bath. I do an immune boosting routine once a week where I soak in the tub for ten to fifteen minutes, then have a cold shower for fifteen to sixty seconds, then turn the shower hot, then cold. You can repeat this in the shower, alternating between the two, and finishing with the cold cycle.

Do something you love

Take time to yourself. If you need to take time off away from work and the everyday stresses of life, then do it. Make the time to heal yourself, by doing the things you enjoy most. I love to be outside. It really fuels my soul. It doesn't matter what time of year it is; you can find me outside. I had participated in this challenge during the month of October. When I completed this challenge, I spent the entire day outside. I went for a hike and a bike ride. I cleaned up my garden. I decorated my house for Halloween. I enjoyed an outing to the pumpkin patch with my sister and nephews. I finished my day by making a video of all the wonderful things I accomplished that day and posted it to my social media page. It was a damp, rainy day, yet I spent the entire day outside. Do something that makes you happy. *What fuels your soul?*

Save $5 a day starting today until the end of the challenge

I bought a piggy bank and put $5 away each day. However, you can just transfer a set amount into a savings account, or there are apps that automatically round your purchase to the nearest dollar.

No screen time today

You would be amazed how much you can accomplish in a day when you detach from the land of social media. Detaching from mainstream media was life-changing. Covid no longer existed in my world. I realized that I wasn't living; I was barely existing. Although I was fully vaccinated, Covid tested daily, and wore a mask with a shield to go to work, I no longer lived my life in fear. I live my life with no regrets.

Go for a walk or hike and connect with nature

Observe your surroundings. Feel, smell, taste, and listen to what is going on around you. Take this time to absorb and bathe in the beauty of Mother Nature. Detach, turn off your phone, relax, be present in the moment.

Oil Pulling

Oil pulling is a technique used for dental hygiene purposes. It's very simple: you put a tablespoon of coconut oil in your mouth and swish it around for twenty minutes. Spit the oil into the garbage and not in the sink or toilet.

My personal experience with oil pulling was a positive one. I had really bad gingivitis, as well as had to have skin grafting done to my gums. I started oil pulling after I had dental surgery. My specialist couldn't believe how my gum line seemed to not only be healing but growing back. My gums are now healthy. I have really white teeth and have never had a cavity. Try oil pulling to see if it's right for you.

Forgive your past and let it go

It's one thing to say I forgive you. It's another thing to say I forgive you and mean it, plus let it go. *How do you forgive someone you no longer speak with?* How I forgave people was I would go to the lake or river and write on rocks. I wrote peoples name on a rock and would set the intention. I would yell, "I forgive you!" and I would release the hold they still had over me. I would scream, then take a sigh of relief as I felt the energy leave my body. It was also important to release and forgive with positive energy. Say, "With love and light I release the hold you have on me." I would wish all the best to those who caused me pain and inflicted trauma on me in the past. I would wish them nothing but love and happiness in this lifetime. I realized that if I held a grudge or released them with hate, it wasn't benefiting my soul's growth. It would only deplete my energy and lower my energetic vibration.

I did this multiple times for the same people until I no longer felt anxious to be around them. I no longer feared running into them in public. This was how I released things I was keeping stored within me energetically. I also forgave myself for the guilt I was hanging onto from everything that had happened throughout my life.

Another good way to release is to write a letter. You don't need to send it to the person. Instead, read the letter out loud as if the person it's concerning is sitting across from you, then burn it and bury the ashes.

EFT therapy (Emotional Freedom Technique therapy) was the only therapy that helped me release on an energetic level.

Pay it forward

Pay it forward is when you do something nice for a stranger with no expectation of them doing anything for you in return. There are many times I will pay for the person behind me in a drive-thru or take a special treat to work for those living in long-term care.

On the day I completed this challenge, I unexpectedly spoke to someone who was homeless. He wouldn't take any money or let me buy him food. Instead, I sat and listened to his story. I let him use my phone to call his daughter. It was very heartwarming. It's amazing that something so small and simple can make such a huge impact on someone's life. He called me an earth angel. That night on my way home, I stopped to pick up a pizza. To my surprise, the person ahead of me paid for my pizza. I also found $111.10 that day that I forgot I had hidden in my house. These are the moments that I am most grateful for. This was truly an amazing day filled with unexpected gifts from the universe.

Take a different route to all your destinations today

Take a different direction to get where you need to go. Even if it's just to take one extra block or go down a different street to get to your final destination. The day I did this, I added an extra ten minutes to my drive. When I arrived home, there was a full rainbow over the house across the street from me. If I hadn't taken that extra scenic route, I would have missed out on seeing this beautiful rainbow.

Talk to a stranger

Personally, I have no stranger danger. I am an extrovert and talk to everyone. So, I needed to challenge myself a little more with this one. This was the day I reached out to a creator on social media who had a large following. I asked if they would be willing to go live and duet with me so I could share my story in front of a larger audience. To my surprise, this person agreed to help me. Imagine someone who had 1.1M followers helping me, someone who had just hit 1K followers. An hour into our live chat, I realized there were 1.5K people watching the live stream. I felt excited to be sharing my story, but in the same breath, I was terrified. I didn't know who was watching. I feared that my ex was going to see me speaking live about promoting my story. I realized that I needed to let this fear go. I was no longer that person I once was. He no longer had any involvement in my current life. We were officially divorced, and I heard through the grapevine that he was getting re-married. I am so grateful that this creator allowed me to go live with them. I overcame some huge internal fears that I didn't even realize I was still holding on to. *I am now free of those fears!*

Compliment everyone you see

I didn't realize how guarded the world has become. As I am writing this, we are almost at the two-year mark since the Covid pandemic first started. I never dreamed in a million years that it would have come to this. At this point in time, masks are mandatory, so everyone I complimented was wearing a mask. I complimented everyone at work on something and most replied with a "thank you." That night after work, I had some errands to run. I complimented everyone I saw, but the message wasn't well received. Many would look down and away from me, as if they didn't hear me or were pretending to look at their phone. *What kind of world are we living in? When did everyone become so cold and distant? What are we teaching the next generation?*

Declutter and get rid of things you no longer use

I went through every closet, drawer, and dresser. I donated, sold, and threw away garbage bags full of stuff. When we declutter and purge things we no longer need or use, it feels good on the inside. I found that I could focus better and felt lighter after my house was organized.

One of my favourite tips is to change the clothes in your closet seasonally. Turn all the hangers to face toward you. After you wear a garment and go to put it away, flip the hanger so it's facing away from you. When the season comes to an end and you switch your wardrobe, anything that has the hanger still facing toward you should be sold or donated. If you didn't wear it for one full season, odds are you won't wear it again.

Dance and sing throughout the day

I like to put on music from different decades as well as different genres.

> *"You've gotta dance like there's nobody watching;*
> *Love like you'll never be hurt; Sing like there's nobody*
> *listening; And live like it's heaven on earth."*
> William W. Purkey

Go to bed early

Ideally, an adult should get a minimum of seven to eight hours of uninterrupted sleep per night. Pick what time works for you. I normally go to bed at 10 p.m. and wake up at 6 a.m.

> *"Early to bed and early to rise, makes a*
> *man healthy, wealthy and wise."*
> Benjamin Franklin

Try a new exercise

I encourage you to try a new activity that pushes you outside of your comfort zone. My new favourite exercise is paddle boarding. I invested in a paddle board but had a fear of falling in the water or looking silly in front of others. I gained the courage to try paddle board yoga for the first time this past summer and fell in love with it. You never know until you try. Since it was now October, it was too cold for paddle board yoga in Canada. I tried something called Piloxing on a DVD that I had bought at a fitness convention years ago. It was a lot of fun!

Make a meal you have never made before

For this challenge, I made Pad Thai at home. I used brown rice noodles with a Thai sauce. I added bean sprouts, broccoli, chives, jumbo shrimp, chopped peppers, and topped it off with some chopped walnuts. It turned out delicious, and it was easy to make, so now I make it on a regular basis.

Write down ten things to manifest into your life

I have been manifesting so many great things into my reality. My current house couldn't be more perfect since I drew this house in my dream journal when I was a child. The thing with manifestation is you set the intention of what you want and then let it go. By doing these things I have outlined in this challenge on a regular basis, you will slowly raise your energy to attract the life of your dreams into reality. I have a chapter in my first book on manifesting. I started to manifest small things into my life to start. Know that if something's not coming to fruition, it is in your highest interest to let go of the outcome and move forward. If it's meant to be, it will be. Let go of the outcome, the how and the when. A couple bigger things that I manifested into my life were:

- **My house:** I drew my current home in my dream journal when I was kid. It had everything my current home has except a pool.

- **A pool:** My neighbour was getting rid of their pool and gave it to me for free.
- **Money:** I found an envelope of money in the junk drawer, money in my coat pocket, and I found a scratch ticket on the ground while walking the dog. The ticket wasn't scratched yet. When I scratched the ticket, I discovered I had won $50. I traded it in for a few more tickets. By the end of the day, I had won over $200 which I cashed in. My hydro bill had a $200 credit on it which lasted almost three months before I needed to pay again.

Do something nice for a family member or friend

My sister is a single mom. I surprised her by arranging for my mom to watch her kids. I booked a hotel and planed a two-day getaway for us to go to a Scandinavian spa. We had a great time, and it was something she wasn't expecting.

Get dressed up and go out for dinner

While on our little getaway, we stayed at a really nice ski village. We went to a fancy restaurant and splurged. I normally wouldn't pay $150 for one meal, but it was well worth it. Sometimes, you have to forget about the cost and think more about the memories that you're making. You can't take money with you when you leave this world. It's the memories that we make and the imprint we leave behind that matters.

Do something out of your comfort zone

While completing this challenge, I did a lot of things that pushed me outside my comfort zone. On this day, I joined an online dating app. That was very scary for me, as I was once married and trapped in an abuse cycle for so long. I was still energetically connected with my twin flame. Although we had no communication in the real world, I could still feel him always. *How could I move on knowing that I was still energetically connected to this other person?* But I knew it was time to move on with my life. So, I joined a random dating app. Within less than twenty-four hours, I had over four hundred messages. It was quite the ego boost. Yet I felt overwhelmed. I picked one person and said let's just meet. No texting, no small talk, just meet. *Guess what?* He agreed to meet me without even knowing who I was. He was a really nice person, but I felt no spark. I am off the dating apps again. The more I focus on me, the more I know that "Mr. Right" will come into my life in some serendipitous way when I least expect it.

Call a friend or family member on the phone

I find it easier to talk on the phone than over text. I call people on a daily basis. On this day, I phoned a friend who I hadn't spoken to in years. We chatted for well over an hour and made plans to get together. We had a great girl's night a few weeks later.

Congratulations! You have completed 30 days! Treat yourself to a reward, you deserve it!

I treated myself to an extra massage this month. I always book one massage a month, but this month I had budgeted for two. My massage therapist also does Reiki energy healing while she massages. She's the best massage therapist I've ever had, and I'm so grateful for her.

Warning! Pay attention to any energy healing professionals you allow to work within your energy field. If they are vibrating at a lower energy level, they can actually do more harm than good. Take precaution with who you let into your energetic bubble.

Keep the challenge going!
Come up with your own challenge
ideas to keep you motivated!
Continue to fuel your soul, you're doing great!

CHAPTER TWO

How to Heal from
Past Trauma

Let's start at the beginning . . .

I was born into a family where my parents were young
when they had me. My dad was a long-distance truck
driver and barley around. When he was around, he was
drunk. My dad was a narcissistic, abusive, angry alcoholic
and very toxic to be around. My parents' relationship
was toxic and unstable. They were together and then not
together so many times throughout my life. I realize now
that my mom was trapped in an abuse cycle.

As a child, I was bullied from elementary school
all the way right through to college. It was as if I were
walking around with a big, bright, flashing neon sign over

my head that said, "pick on me." People who I thought were my friends would make fun of me behind my back. I had a girl come into my Grade 9 math class and pull me out of the room by my hair. She then proceeded to beat me in the hallway. She thought I had kissed her boyfriend. I hadn't even kissed a boy at that stage in my life. I had another traumatic incident where a group of boys shoved me into a locker and locked me inside. Lucky for me, the janitor heard me yelling for help. People I didn't even know would randomly pick on me. Once there was a car of teenagers that followed me as I was walking home from school. They purposely hit every puddle to soak me and were throwing food at me from the car window. They continuously drove past me, driving in circles as I walked. I entered a movie rental store to get away from them. I was covered in pop and ketchup. The owner of the store asked a customer in the store to drive me home. No matter what I did, I always seemed to be the target.

I spent a lot of time isolated by myself. At that stage in my life, I was a shy, quiet, introvert and didn't openly share or express any of what I was experiencing. I went through a rough patch between the ages of fourteen to eighteen when I had suicidal thoughts. Although no one would have ever known it. To the outside world, I looked like a happy-go-lucky, "normal" teenager. While in reality, I was dying inside.

I never had anyone to rely on but myself. I would wait for someone to pick me up from school or an after-school activity, only to have to walk home when neither parent remembered to pick me up. I was told, "You have two feet and a heartbeat, you can walk." My parents reinforced the idea that a ride home was a privilege not a right. They would tell me how great my life was and how lucky I was to have a roof over my head and food on the table. When I did express how I was feeling, they would disregard my feelings. They would say things like, "there are people who are suffering more than you are, think of all those starving kids in Africa, suck it up." It would have been nice if they would have cared and acknowledged how I felt, instead of brushing it off. I had expressed to both my parent how this was not the response I was hoping for, and that I would like my feelings to be acknowledged.

After years of therapy, I came to the realization that, my parents don't realize the impact this has had on my mental health. I had spent so many years being devalued. No wonder I lost my sense of self-worth. Today I just keep setting my boundaries and re-enforcing the fact that, I don't like how my feelings are ignored. I have asked them to please stop comparing me to someone living in a third world country. I have asked them to listen to how I'm actually feeling. I have come to the realization that I need to accept the fact that this behaviour will never change. If I want to continue to have a relationship with my mom, I need to accept that this is just her way of speaking to me. I cut my dad out of my life over fifteen years ago, as he had overstepped a lot more boundaries.

On my sixteenth birthday, my dad left permanently. He moved directly from our house to living with another lady, replacing us with his new family. From that day forward, I was an adult. My mom was a struggling single parent as he had just walked away. I was told that I needed to pay $100 a week to live at home, along with my own groceries and car insurance. I was also responsible for anything extra that I wanted like clothes. I worked three jobs while I also paid my way through college.

As I got older, I would make plans to meet up with my dad, only to get stood up. He would then apologize later for forgetting about me. This was where my abandonment issues stemmed from. I normalized this behaviour as well as the abuse.

When I was eighteen years old, I snuck into a night club with a fake ID. Someone bought me a drink. I ended up drugged and date raped. I remember feeling as if I were on a tilt-a-whirl. Everything was spinning. I don't know how I went from being at a night club to some guy's bed. I remember being in and out of consciousness, trying to say no and push him off me. I remember waking up the next morning naked in this stranger's bed. I had no clue where I was or how I got there. I didn't know where my friends had disappeared to, where my purse was, or how I was going to get home. I snuck out of this person's home and walked until I found a payphone. I was able to make a collect call. I wasn't even in the same city as the night club nor was I in the city that I lived in. I took a taxi home and sat in the bathtub crying while the water poured down from the showerhead, immersing my entire body. I felt so dirty. I didn't know what to do, I was alone and scared. I walked to the Sexual Healthcare Clinic where I was examined, took the morning-after pill and was tested for different STDs. I also had to make a police report. Everything was confidential. As I was over the age of eighteen, they didn't notify my parents. The only other person I told this to was my therapist, many years later. That would be the story as to how I lost my virginity.

After I was raped, I continued to attract people into my life who used me. I was the side chick, or they only used me for sex. I had little self-worth. I was just happy someone was paying attention to me. Reflecting back on my life from childhood into adulthood, it is no surprise that I went on to marry someone who was narcissistic, controlling, and abusive.

I have held onto these memories for far too many years. It feels good to share as I know there are other people out there who have experienced these same types of situations and can relate. It helps to know that you are not alone.

I had years of anger and resentment stored within me! How did I heal from years of trauma?

Warning! Research has shown that the suppression of emotions can cause illness to manifest in the physical body. I have had many personal experiences to support this theory. While reprocessing sexual trauma in therapy, I had a large cyst rupture on my right ovary. I had never experienced so much pain in my life and went septic. I was hospitalized!

The cyst is only one example. I have my own saying which is, "mental crap makes belly fat." The more I released things that I had held onto energetically, the more the bloating in my belly went down. I lost weight in a healthy way. The pain in my neck and shoulders subsided. My menstrual cycles started to regulate and become lighter. I had more energy.

Processing anger

What I've learned throughout the years is that if someone is arguing with you, it's best not to argue back. Stay cool, calm and collected before responding in an irrational way. Speak to the person who has made you angry in the heat of the moment or give yourself time to cool off before confronting the problem. Don't take your anger out on someone else. Don't bottle up or hold onto the emotion, release it in that moment. Holding a grudge and staying angry with someone destroys all that is beautiful within you. Release it with positive love and light.

Techniques I use to release stored anger:

- *Screaming*
- *Punching a pillow*
- *Singing and dancing to loud music*
- *Tearing up paper*
- *Breathing techniques*
- *Burning letters*
- *Talking about it (therapy)*
- *Writing down my feelings*
- *Throwing rocks*

Draw or paint how you feel:

- *What shape is anger?*
- *What colour is it?*
- *Does it have a texture?*
- *What does its environment look like?*
- *Where is the anger located in the body?*

Mantra to release bottled up emotions

I release all tension, fear, anger, guilt, and sadness.
I accept and release my past to create a
better reality for my future self.
I let go of old beliefs and limitations.
I allow for peace and love to flow freely
through my entire being.
I am at peace with the process of life.
I know that I am unconditional universal love and light.

Learning to forgive

Not only did I need to forgive others for the pain that they had inflicted on me over the years, I needed to forgive myself for holding on to the trauma. For a long time, I felt guilty for the way I left my ex-husband. I knew what was happening, but from an outsider's perspective, it looked as if I hugged someone and left my husband. When in reality, I had all this weird stuff happening to me. My DNA was upgrading at an alarming rate on an energetic soul level. I was already contemplating leaving him before the awakening happened.

Once again, EFT (Emotional Freedom Technique therapy) really helped. My therapist would have me close my eyes and visualize a safe place. My safe place was a beach. We would slowly reprocess memories that I had stored and didn't know I was still holding on to. I highly recommend this type of therapy for anyone who has found themselves suffering from anxiety, depression or PTSD.

I was also doing something called dissociation where instead of talking about what was wrong in the moment, I would bottle it up and store it away. On the outside, I would walk around with a happy face and pretend as if nothing was wrong. Realistically, I was suffering internally. I went on auto pilot and failed to actually feel my emotions. *It's okay to not be okay.* It's okay to cry and feel your emotions. It was good for me to cry and release all my stored emotions.

I realized that I needed to forgive my parents for the traumatic events that took place throughout my life. They were young. They didn't know what they were doing as they were just kids themselves. I know that they did the best job they could under the circumstances. They have their own wounds and life experiences that they must process in their own way. I still love and respect them for their life choices, but that doesn't mean that their way of life has any impact on the way I live my life today. I accept them both for who they are. I choose not to have a relationship with my father and have released him with love and light.

I used the techniques previously mentioned to release the stored guilt and anger so I could forgive. I realized that I didn't have to approach my abusers to forgive them. I just needed to make peace with it within myself. These techniques also work if you're lacking closure from any situation. Make peace with it within yourself, and you will stop longing for validation or an apology from an outside source. I have written letters to my abusers. Which I didn't send, I would pretend to read them to my abuser then burn the letter. I then write a return letter back to myself apologizing for their actions. I have also done this through text, I text back and forth with myself, as if I'm texting with the person who I would like to speak too. This has helped me move forward in my own life without the expectation of them reaching out. It was another way that I received closure.

> *"To forgive is to set a prisoner free and discover that the prisoner was you."*
> Lewis B. Smedes

How I released my twin flame

I struggled for far too long with releasing the intense connection I shared with my twin flame. Even though he had blocked and ghosted me out of his life, I spent an exponential amount of time fantasizing about our future together. It was weird how easy it was for him to let me go and just walk away from the connection. As if I never existed. I, on the other hand, tried everything to release this hold he had on me, but nothing worked.

> *How was I going to release my twin flame?*
> *We are one, one soul in two bodies.*
> *How do you release someone who is*
> *you on an energetic soul level?*

What I did was I held a funeral. If he was going to ghost me, then I was going to treat him like a ghost. I wrote a eulogy, bought flowers, and lit some candles. It felt as if he were actually dead. I wrote the eulogy inside a sympathy card. I burned it and buried the ashes in the garden. In memory of him, I then placed a light pink-coloured rose quartz crystal in the garden on top of the ashes. I cried like I had never cried before.

Afterwards, I felt relieved. I had finally surrendered to the connection. I had let go of the physical version of him and was finally free.

There was no him now, there was just me. By doing this, I was able to detach from the physical aspect of him coming back into my life. This in turn allowed me to move forward without the expectation of him being present in my life. This works to detach from all different situations. If you're feeling as if you have no closure to a situation or someone has blocked you, I highly recommend releasing it through a mock funeral.

Eulogy for my twin flame

Reflecting on the time we shared together, it makes me so happy to have had you as a friend in my life. That weekend we shared together was like magic. It was something out of a fairy tale. I will cherish that short period of time we spent together for the rest of my life. I keep reminding myself that life is not a Cinderella story, and not every story has a happily ever after. When you kissed me, I felt fireworks within my entire being. I had never felt anything like that before, and I will never experience that again. I thank you so much for that moment. For in that moment, my heart chakra was wide open, and I felt the burning love that you're supposed to feel for someone.

If I had three wishes:

I wish you knew the depth of this connection.
I wish we could have communicated more.
I wish you knew how much your friendship meant to me.

It was wrong of me to have overwhelmed you by sharing all the weird crazy stuff that was happening to me. I thought that I was cursed as I watched my entire life fall apart. I thought that you would understand where I was coming from, since we triggered this together. I assumed you were experiencing what I was. I was wrong, and I am sorry.

I am so grateful you took the time out of your weekend to listen to my side of the story. Instead of calling me crazy, you pulled me in closer and supported me. Thank you!

How did you not feel the fireworks between us?

I didn't know what love was until I hugged you. I will forever be grateful for that hug we shared. For that was the hug that gave me back my life. I know life has not been easy for you. Trust me, I've been there too. Our lives mirror and reflect one another.

My hope and wish for you is that you are happy wherever you are. I hope you live a long and prosperous life filled with love and joyous moments. I hope you find someone to share your life with even if that isn't me. I wish you nothing but the best in this lifetime. Know that I love and support you always and forever.

> *"It's better to have loved and lost than*
> *never to have loved at all."*
> Alfred Lord Tennyson

I normalized people not showing up for me, but in reality, I was sending that energy to the universe. I always had this fear that I was going to get stood up, let down or abandoned. So that was exactly what I attracted into my life. It wasn't until after I shifted my mindset, started showing up for myself, and reprocessed my internal abandonment issues from childhood that I realized how the only person I can really count on to show up for me in this lifetime is me.

I let go of the fear of people not showing up for me. If someone doesn't show up to meet me, oh well, it's their loss. That doesn't stop me from enjoying a dinner out at a restaurant or participating in an activity by myself. Although I may be alone, I am never lonely. I am actually the best company for myself. I know how to meet all my needs to sustain a happy, healthy relationship.

> *"The most important relationship you have in*
> *life is the one you have with yourself."*
> Diane von Furstenberg

I started to heal the abandonment issues through reprocessing my core issues that I didn't even know were there. I learned how to nurture my inner child by using visualization techniques through meditation and dream state. I used meditation techniques and visualized hugging my younger self. I nurtured her, showering her with the love and care that she deserved as a child.

I started showing up for myself and fueling my own soul. I now take myself out on regular date nights and send myself flowers with loving cards attached. I buy myself little gifts and wrap them up for special occasions. The more I love myself, the more I let go of the need to be with someone else to make me happy. I learned that you can't be dependent on someone for your happiness.

I honestly had never experienced true love before I hugged my twin flame. Love is not a word that you say to someone. *Love is a feeling!* It was only then that I felt love for the first time at the age of thirty-four. I then came to the realization that you can't just hug someone and ride off into the sunset with them just because they hold the other half of your soul. The purpose of the twin flame connection is to heal within yourself on a soul level.

This is the love you're supposed to feel for yourself!

Love feels like a safe home; it also feels like fireworks. I look in the mirror and know that I am so beautiful inside and out. No one can stop me now. There's a bonfire burning within my heart and soul; it's an unconditional love for myself that I never knew existed.

I LOVE MYSELF!

How did I do it?
How did I get to a point where I feel this unconditional love for myself?

I worked on three things:
self-love
self-confidence
self-worth

Self-Love

I loved myself enough to leave my entire life behind. I took a risk to walk out that door and start over. I left my abuser, I started doing activities that I enjoyed, and I took care of myself by eating foods that fueled my body in a healthy way while exercising daily. I started living life in the moment and not worrying about past trauma or future events. I stopped caring what others thought of me. I march to the beat of my own drum. I love and accept who I am in the present moment, flaws and all.

Think about when you're on an airplane and they're going over the safety tips. They say to put your oxygen mask on first before helping others. We need to remember that it's not selfish to put ourselves first. Take the time to rest, to care and nurture yourself. It's important to put yourself first, so in return, you will be in a better position to help others.

If you can't help yourself, who can you help?
Do you treat yourself the way you treat others?
Are you comfortable in your own skin?
Would you be friends with you?

The truth is that if you can't love yourself, how can someone love you in the way you deserve to be loved?

Self-Confidence

When I first started this journey, I was lost, confused, scared, and broken. I felt as if no one would ever love me or want to be with me. I wasn't comfortable in my own skin. I focused on every flaw I could find with my physical body. My ex had belittled me for so long, and had I believed all the horrible things he had said about me.

I also felt abandoned by my twin flame who had just cut me out of his life. He woke up one day and decided, *that's it. I'm going to pretend as if none of this ever happened and walk away from the connection.*

I totally lost my self-confidence. I had these two men who wanted to be with me. Then within a few months' time, neither one wanted to be with me and abandoned me. Then I realized that I had abandoned myself. I was seeking love, support and validation from them. I needed to learn how to trust again. The first person I needed to learn to trust was myself.

How do I trust?

Life holds many lessons. Everyone comes into our lives for a reason, whether it's for a season or a lifetime. We play a role in the lives of everyone we come into contact with. I believe that roadblocks are placed on our path for healing purposes.

> *"Life doesn't happen to you; it happens for you."*
> Tony Robbins

There were times throughout this process that I had no clue what direction my life was headed. I just had faith that there was a divine plan in place, although, I didn't know the end result. I knew that no matter what, I had trust that my higher self, guides, angels, universe and the divine had my back.

I know that no matter what the outcome is, I will always be exactly where I need to be in that moment.

If you can't trust yourself, who can you trust? How did I regain my self-confidence?

I started reading the affirmations in the mirror and truly started to believe them. I listened to mantras. I would make up fun songs and sing to myself.

"Oh, you beautiful soul! You great, big, beautiful soul! Let me put my arms around you, I could never live without you. Oh, you beautiful soul! You great, big, beautiful soul! If you ever leave me how my heart would ache, I want to hug you but I fear you'd break. Oh, oh, oh, oh, oh, you beautiful soul!"
(sung to the tune of "Oh, You Beautiful Doll" by Seymour Brown).

I started public speaking and making videos, sharing my story with the world. I would get dressed up and do my hair and makeup. I would write myself love letters and take myself out on fancy date nights. This went hand in hand with building my self-worth.

Self-Worth

I worked on my self-worth by showing up for myself. If no one was going to show up for me, I was going to show up for myself. I discovered that I am accountable for my own thoughts and actions toward myself. I became that loving person who I thought was missing from my life. I know my worth, and I can feel it. I know that I am a strong, amazing, independent woman who can achieve anything I want in life. I am good enough, I am fearless, and I am capable of accomplishing everything I put my mind to. I had a sign custom-made which is my new moto that I live by. It says:

Wish it, dream it, believe it, achieve it!

"One day, your heart with stop beating,
and none of your fears will matter.
All that will matter is how you lived."
Henri Junttila

CHAPTER THREE

How to Leave an Abuse Cycle

Prior to my awakening, I didn't even realize that I was trapped in an abuse cycle. I normalized it, as I had grown up in an abuse cycle. I didn't realize that there was anything wrong with the way my husband treated me. I would make up excuses for my husband's behaviour. In my first book, I wrote more in-depth about the abuse I endured. I kept it pretty PG in terms of what actually happened.

I recently came across this letter I had written to myself. I remember how I was feeling in the moment. I was crying so bad that I couldn't see through the tears, and as I put pen to paper, all the emotion poured out.

Here is some of what I wrote in October 2019 . . .

Abuse

A healthy relationship is one in which you and your partner feel free to express what hurts, scares and worries you. You must also feel comfortable to share your deepest darkest secrets with one another as well as your hopes and dreams. An emotional abuser doesn't want to hear about your pain, except to reinforce that you deserve whatever pain you feel. They reinforce that you've brought it on yourself and that you deserve to feel bad.

My husband made me feel as if everything was always my fault. It was my fault that he was hurting. If we had a fight, it was always my fault, either I started it or triggered it somehow. I tried to explain to him what was happening to me, and he made me feel as if I were crazy.

Honestly, I still couldn't believe that I hugged someone, and then suddenly, was seeing my life in a completely different light. I tried to explain the awakening to my husband. I told him that I needed time alone to process what was happening to me. I was so scared. I didn't know how to navigate a spiritual awakening. Maybe he was right, maybe I was crazy, maybe I did belong in a mental institution.

He kept flipping everything around as if it were my fault. Apparently, he couldn't eat or sleep because I had broken him so bad. He was so depressed that he kept threatening that if I didn't go home, he would just kill himself. I understood that he was upset with me leaving. He was doing and saying everything he could to get me to go back home. The problem was that he didn't see the problem. He didn't even try to understand my feelings. He turned it all around as if he was the one suffering.

What happened to my needs?
What about my feelings?
What about what I was experiencing?

It wasn't fair to stay in a loveless marriage. He deserved to be with his soulmate, which I knew wasn't me. I wanted him to find someone who complimented his lifestyle. He was a fifteen-year-old boy trapped in a thirty-eight-year-old body. He spent the majority of his time playing video games, drinking and over indulging in drugs. My husband in this lifetime was my son in a previous lifetime. Once I woke up to this fact, I no longer felt any sexual desire to be with him. I knew that I needed to leave! The karmic cycle had run its course.

Control

I was no longer allowed to go out with friends or make plans that didn't involve him. He had cameras installed inside and outside the house and would monitor where I was at all times. If my car wasn't in the driveway, he would text me. If I didn't answer my text, he would call. He was logged into my messenger account and was monitoring everyone I was in communication with. He kept track of my every move. He would question who I was speaking to and accused me of having sex with random people.

<u>My husband would say things like:</u>

- *No one would ever want you.*
- *I'm the only one for you.*
- *No one will love you like I do.*
- *No one will take care of you the way I do.*
- *You won't be able to survive without my finances.*
- *You would be stupid to leave.*
- *We are almost mortgage-free.*
- *You're not allowed to leave me, we're married.*

He kept trying to convince me that my life with him was perfect. He had me brainwashed, and so I believed that I couldn't make it on my own. I felt that I would never be good enough for anyone but him.

He was wrong!

When I finally did get the courage to leave, I tried to set boundaries. He would disrespect them. I needed a break from him to figure out what I wanted out of life. I had asked him not to text, call, or contact my friends or family members. He would disrespect me. I received well over a hundred texts with over fifty missed calls per day. He even called my mom, sister, and nana when I wouldn't answer. I just wanted to be left alone!

How could I figure out if I really missed him or not if he wouldn't give me time to myself?

When I didn't respond, he showed up at my work with flowers. He told my coworkers that I was being unreasonable and needed to go home. When he was asked to leave the property, he refused. He was escorted out of my work place by my supervisor. He was told that we would call the police if he didn't leave. He then proceeded to wait out in the parking lot, with a beautiful bouquet of flowers, until I finished work. I spoke with him briefly. He begged me to go home. He convinced me to go home for the weekend. I quickly realized that I had gone home for the wrong reasons. I went home because he made me feel guilty, not because I wanted to.

My husband controlled the money. His money was his money, and my money was our money. Although he made a lot more than I did, we paid for everything 50/50. After I left, I realized that I had been paying well over 50% of my fair share.

I didn't know where his money went!

I never had access to his bank statements. The one time I used his card to put gas in my car, he called the bank, saying that there was fraudulent activity on his account. Meanwhile, I thought we were married, meaning it was our money. Apparently, I was wrong, and that was the one and only time I ever used his debit card.

He tried to buy my love back with a new outfit, bowling, dinner out, stocking the fridge, etc. He even offered to book a trip to a destination of my choice. All so I would come home. This was not the right way to get me to go home. These tactics had always worked in the past, but this time was different.

I told him that he had to find a therapist and book an appointment, or I was never going home. He made it clear that I would be the one paying since I was the one wanting to go to therapy.

My breaking point

I tried to share with my husband how I was feeling and what I needed. One final time. Instead of listening, he got very dramatic. He threw himself on the floor, stating that he couldn't breathe. *(He reminded me of a little kid being left at daycare).* He put his fingers in his mouth to trigger him to throw up. He started to punch himself in the face, trying to give himself two black eyes. I continued to ignore him. Normally, I would have comforted him, but this time was different.

He told me that he had to go to the hospital because he couldn't breathe. He claimed that he was having a heart attack, and if I left him for good, he would die. I reassured him that he wasn't going to die. I kept trying to explain that I just needed some time to process what was happening to me. I needed at least another week or two to gather my thoughts.

He panicked as he was losing the control he had over me. He said that if I left him again that he would kill himself. As I went to walk out the door, he tried to stop me. He grabbed a knife from the kitchen. He stood there holding the knife. He cornered me in the kitchen and said, "If I can't have you no, one will." He held the knife closer to my throat. I did become concerned for my well-being. I knew that I needed to leave, and it was now or never. I called his bluff and pushed my way past him. He looked at me in awe. As I went to walk out the door, he chased after me and handed me the knife. He said, "On second thought, if I can't have you, life isn't worth living. You kill me, that way you will go to jail and the blood will be on your hands."

That was the moment I felt the energetic release. I was so done. I walked out that door for the last time that night.

What I discovered after I left:

- *I was no longer in love with my husband.*
- *I had knots in my stomach when I went home.*
- *I felt like I was going to throw up when I was around him.*
- *I was on pins and needles in my own home.*
- *I was not comfortable being around him.*
- *When I went home, I had no energy. I could just crawl into bed and sleep for days.*
- *I was better on the days I didn't hear from him.*
- *I felt peace within myself the more I stayed away from him.*
- *I had more energy when I didn't see him.*
- *I was getting my spark back.*
- *I had more motivation.*

- *I was going out with friends again.*
- *I was going to the gym daily.*
- *I was really enjoying this new version of me that I was becoming!*

I was feeling so much better in taking time to myself and focusing on my own well-being. It had been fourteen years of this. We had lots of good times, but now the bad were outweighing the good.

It was time to move on!

I knew that my husband was not capable of changing in the ways that I needed him to. Nor should I have expected him to change who he was for me. We were living two completely different lives in one household. We had different life goals. As scary as it was to leave behind fourteen years of friendship, memories, and a life I once knew, I realized that I needed to leave for my own well-being and mental health. I could no longer rely on him to support me.

I definitely hit my breaking point. The last two fights had been really bad. My husband would say it was never physical as he never physically hit me. Regardless, reflecting back on how he treated me, it was not right. Even if he didn't physically hit me directly, he still got upset, hit things and yelled at me. This last fight I just described was the fight that pushed me over the edge. That was the fight that ended it all.

I had tried to explain my needs to my husband multiple times. He would never understand my point of view. It was always about what he wanted. He was still head over heels in love with me. I was obviously not feeling the love. When I said that I didn't want to be hugged or kissed, he did it anyways. I told him that I didn't want to have sex. He forced me by pushing me onto the bed and pinning me down. I felt as if he raped me as I just laid there and let him take advantage of my body. Reflecting back, I now recognize that I was trapped in an abuse cycle!

How to recognize that you are trapped in an abuse cycle

1) **The honeymoon phase**
   All seems well. This is "normal" life.
2) **Tension builds**
   Tempers start to heighten. The victim can feel the energy shift and feels as if they are walking on eggshells. The victim tries to stay on their best behaviour, careful not to trigger an explosion.

3) **Explosion (abuse happens)**
   Mental abuse, physical abuse, sexual abuse, financial abuse. Regardless of the abuse, it's abuse, and this is the explosion.

4) **Apologies and gifts**
   The abuser apologizes for their actions and begs for the victim to come back. The abuser buys the victim gifts and promises it's going to be different. They say they won't do it again, and that they have changed their ways.

5) **Repeat**
   The victim returns home, and the entire cycle repeats again. It might be days, weeks, months or even a year later, but the abuser goes back to their old ways, and the cycle repeats itself again.

How to break the cycle

Step 1: Recognize that you're trapped in an abuse cycle.

Step 2: Make an action plan to leave in a safe way. Talk to a police officer, lawyer, therapist, friends and family. Contact your local women's shelter.

Step 3: Leave when the abuser is not home.

Step 4: Stay strong and don't go back.

Step 5: Take back the power and control of your own life.

There were many times before my awakening that I would leave when things escalated and then go back. I go more in-depth about my personal struggles with leaving and getting sucked back into the abuse cycle in my first book. Over the course of fourteen years, I lost count of how many times I went back to this same cycle. I know how hard it was to break the cycle. No one deserves to be abused or controlled on any level.

I am so proud of myself for having the courage to finally leave and not go back. Although I did try and make my marriage work multiple times, I was more than done by the time I walked out that door for the last time.

I realized that I could replace things, but I couldn't replace my mental health. I made a pros and cons list regarding leaving my husband as well as asking myself many questions throughout this process.

<u>Questions I asked myself before I made my final decision</u>

- *What is my reason for staying?*
- *How did it make me feel when I went home?*

- *Where am I going to go?*
- *Where am I going to live temporarily?*
- *What is my long-term plan?*
- *How can I heal if I stay in the same cycle?*
- *Can I really spend the rest of my life living like this?*
- *Am I really living or just settling?*
- *When did my wants and desires become unimportant?*
- *How am I actually feeling?*
- *What do I desire to feel?*
- *When did I lose the power and control over my own life?*
- *Why did I give someone else the power and control over my life?*
- *How long have I let my husband control me like this?*
- *How have I let someone else make me feel so bad about myself?*
- *How can I stay in a loveless marriage?*
- *Is it worth the time and effort to work on our marriage?*
- *Will anything change?*
- *How can I financially afford to do this on my own?*
- *How do I leave in a safe way?*
- *What will make me happy?*
- *What can I do to change my current situation?*
- *What do I want for myself in this lifetime?*
- *What is my life's purpose?*

If you recognize that you're trapped in an abuse cycle and don't know how to break free in a safe way, I suggest you reach out for help.

> ***You always have the power and
> control over your own life!***

CHAPTER FOUR

How to Live Life in the Now

I work with individuals with Alzheimer's disease and other forms of dementia. My job actually sparked my realization that the twin flame obsession is very similar to those who are sundowning. These individuals walk around, wandering the halls day in and out, asking to go home. Every thirty seconds, they ask to go home. Although they are home, in their mind, they are looking to go back to their childhood home.

You see the brain is like an onion. An onion has layers. For example, take the centre core of the onion. The core is where you find your memories from childhood. You remember your mom, dad, sister, brother, childhood home, school, and things you used to enjoy doing. As we age, the brain (or onion so to speak) gains more layers. You grow up, graduate high school, get married, buy a house, have children and grandchildren. The layers build every day until the onion gets so big and the layers get so weak that we start to lose the outer part of our onion. That's why someone with Alzheimer's disease can't remember what they did just a few short minutes ago but instead are obsessively in search of their parents and childhood home. They have reverted back in time in their brain, back to the core memories. (I often wonder if this is the process of the soul clearing the memories from this lifetime for when it reincarnates into its next life?)

The key to prevent this behaviour is to keep the individual engaged in an activity that they enjoy. For example, exercise, painting, puzzles, sing along or bingo. There are many activities to choose from. During the activity, the individual is so engaged with what is going on in that present moment, and so they completely forget that they were looking to go home. They may not remember the activity minutes after participating, but the important part is that they were present in that moment while the activity was taking place.

So now you may ask, what does this have anything to do with me learning to be present in the moment? What does this have to do with the twin flame obsession? It has everything to do with it . . .

We are made up of three parts: body, mind and soul. We always have the control over our own body and mind, but in the twin flame dynamic, you are one soul, and the soul is what you are. So the soul is constantly looking to go "home." Now that you have recognized your soul inside of another human being, it's constantly looking to go "home." It keeps you constantly in search of them and wondering about them, which triggers the mind and the ego. We still have full control of the situation as a human being in a body as you have control of the body and the mind. The soul, however, accelerates to a whole new level after this meeting of its other self.

So how do you control this?
Live your life in the now!

This goes for everyone, not just those on the twin flame journey. Don't worry about the past. It's in the past, and there is nothing you can do about it. This is easier said than done. Try your best to live in the moment. Step into your power and take back the control of your own body and mind. Focus on activities that fuel your soul. I enjoy so many different activities. When you do these things, be present in that moment. Don't waste your time worrying about the past or about what's to come. Just be in that moment. Take a moment to stop to smell the roses, so to speak. Focus on the way you feel in that moment. Stop worrying about things that need to get done, or how other people are affecting your life situation. Pull back your energy and put all the focus back on you.

Now there are times when you are going to be living in the present moment but discussing the past or present. For example, if you are planning for a trip. You are planning for that trip in the present moment, yet that trip will take place at a future date. Same goes for if you are attending a funeral and grieving the loss of a person. It's okay to reminisce in the present moment in order to move forward. The most important takeaway here is to focus on the good times and heal from anything that is holding you back from moving forward. Don't stay trapped in the past. Put the phone away and focus on the activity that is taking place in the present moment. Be sure to engage with those who are physically in your presence instead of being preoccupied with distractions.

A list of some of the activities that I enjoy:

Journaling/Writing
Crafting
Horseback riding
Exercising
Going out with friends
Getting a haircut
Hiking
Going to the cottage
Having a beach day
Going outside
Taking a bath
Volunteering
Biking
Going on a picnic
Going to an amusement park
Swimming
Playing board games
Going to the zoo
Paddle boarding
Bocce Ball
Going to the aquarium
Rollerblading
Bowling
Going to a sporting event
Weight training

Mini-putting
Singing
Go-karting
Practicing yoga
Washing the car
Exploring somewhere new
Meditating
Taking pictures
Getting a manicure/pedicure
Gardening
Watching a movie
Laying in the sunshine
Baking
Playing laser tag
Building a snowman
Cooking
Going on an ATV
Woodworking
Painting
Snowmobiling
Learning to play an instrument
Camping
Having a bonfire
Watching home movies
Fishing

Billiards
Going to the arcade
Dancing
Scrapbooking
Colouring
Travelling
Getting a massage
Renovating the house
Knitting
Playing cards
Decorating
Shopping
Going for a car ride
Cuddling
Flirting
Going to the fair
Going to a concert
Playing a sport
Relax
Cleaning
Hosting a party
Doing a word search
Phoning a friend
Doing a crossword
Listening to music
Watching TV

Getting a makeover
Drawing a picture
Boating
Having a spa day
Going to a national park
Crocheting
Learning something new
Learning tarot
Public speaking
Going live on social media
Meeting new people
Going to a trivia night
Ice skating
Spending time with family
Going to the casino
Going to the drive-in
Mailing Christmas cards
Responding to e-mails
Bird-watching
Laughing/telling jokes
Mowing the lawn
Taking a shower
Spending time alone
Taking myself on a date night
Enjoying life

Chapter Five

How to Protect Your Energy

As an empath, it is important for me to cut energetic cords, shield and protect my energy. I wish I knew of these techniques earlier in life. Once I started mediating, clearing out other people's energy, and using invisible protective energetic bubbles and armour, life became more bearable.

Picture Care Bears when they do the Care Bear Stare. Their rainbow is positive energy. It protects against the negative energy coming at it. Positive energy always wins. We all have our own rainbow of energy within us. Our rainbow is the chakras in the body. The seven main chakras are: the root (red), sacral (orange), solar plexus (yellow), heart (green), throat (blue), third eye (indigo), and crown (white/ dark purple).

We all have our own chakra system. At the end of the day, that's what we are. We are an energetic soul in a meat suit. We are all connected on an energetic level. When we expose ourselves to others, our rainbows all connect to one another. Ever notice how you can be in the best mood, and all it takes is for one negative comment or one negative person to bring you down to their level? *Ever walk into a room full of people and felt the energy?* You can feel who to stay away from and who you're drawn to by their energy. Try your best to stay on a high vibrational frequency.

I also realized that it was important to protect myself when it came to who I let into my bubble. For example, let's talk about sex. I now know that sex an energy exchange between two souls. When we have meaningless sex with multiple partners, it takes a toll on our heart and soul. We consume the energy of not just that one person we slept with but all of their sexual partners (the list can be infinite, depending on how many partners you both have had). That's why one night stands or friends with benefits leave us feeling empty, broken, abandoned, anxious, needy and in a low energetic vibration. Sex should be a sacred energy exchange of pure unconditional love for one another. Only then are you receiving that loving, caring, healing energy from one another and it feels amazing.

I am very cautious as to who I let into my sex life!

How do you cut energetic cords?

Cutting energy cords can be done on a daily basis. I walk around brushing off the energy of others throughout my day. I make pretend scissors and cut the cords away from my chakras.

I have also done full moon rituals where I write the names of those who still have a toxic hold on me energetically. I cover the papers with a release oil. I light them on fire, then put them in a bowl to burn. I stir it up with sage and lemongrass. I imagine burning the connection between these toxic people in my life, instead of just cutting the cords. I imagine burning them and cauterizing the connection so it can't grow back. Then I bury the ashes.

Caution! This works on everyone except for a twin flame connection. You are one soul in two bodies. The soul is energy, and you share a chakra system. That's why the kundalini activation takes place when you connect. The kundalini awakening is the number one sign that this other person is your twin flame. I tried to cut the cords on my twin flame by using this technique, and it bounced back at me. I ended up with bruises and burns all over my physical body. You can tune their energy down a notch by using meditation, but you can't cut the cord. Envision the two of you during meditation. Visualize the two of you tied together with a ribbon. Untangle the ribbon and free yourself from one another. The ribbon tends to come back so do this daily until the connection weakens.

So how do you protect your energy from energy vampires?

How to protect/shield your energy

I use a protective meditation bubble. What I do is before bed, I lay down. I first ground myself by visualizing my feet growing roots and connecting to the centre of the earth. I then go into a meditation where I visualize a white light covering my entire body, protecting me from anything harmful while I sleep. I add a golden sunshine bright net on top of the white bubble of light and visualize it covered in roses. You can create your own safe bubble. Allow only pure LOVE to flow in and out. I have also put a bright white light dome around my room and set the intention that nothing is allowed in my bedroom between 10 p.m. and 6 a.m. If spirit has a message for me, I ask them to put it into one of my dreams. I ask to remember the dream when I wake up. This has been life-changing for me. I am now able to sleep through the night with uninterrupted sleep, but I still receive the messages.

Shielding my energy during the day is similar to what I do before bed. I normally start my day with a sixty-minute exercise program. Then I take what I call a meditation shower. This is where I ground myself and visualize all the negative energy attached to me washing down the drain. I close my eyes and visualize the negative energy within me like black tar oozing out of my body. I see it washing down the drain and turning into a beautiful liquid gold that fuels Mother Earth as it pours out of me. I then ground myself. When I get out of the shower, I dry myself off. As I get dressed, I envision that there is a coat of armour surrounding my clothes. I state the intention that, "I'm rubber, you're glue. Whatever negativity you throw at me bounces off me and comes back to you with love and light."

In my first book, I had mentioned that I used sage to remove negative energy that was within the house I was staying in. One important point that I had failed to mention was that when doing a smudging and using sage, you need somewhere for the energy to go. So open the windows and doors to the outside while doing this as well as a broom to sweep all the negative energy out the door. I still use sage on a regular basis to clear energy.

Chapter Six

How to Identify a Scam

Throughout my own spiritual awakening process, I became very desperate to find answers. I reached out to people who called themselves "twin flame professionals." I won't specify who they are but trust your own intuition if something is a scam or not.

I had people reach out to me over social media. They would say things like:

- ❖ *Hello beautiful soul, your ancestors have an important message for you.*
- ❖ *You have won a free thirty-minute reading. Please enter your e-mail to claim.*

❖ *Your page is amazing, and I would love to work with you. Please contact me for more information.*

❖ *Hi dear, can I please have your name and date of birth? Your angels and guides have a message for you.*

The list goes on and on. I receive messages like these in my inbox on a daily basis. I even had a situation where someone who I am actually friends with contacted me. The message read, "Hello beautiful angel. Sorry to bother you, but my guides are telling me to do a reading for you." It turned out that someone had hacked her account. I thought it was weird that she was reaching out to me like this since I am in communication with her on a regular basis. Instead of responding over social media, I sent her a text. I then reported this person as using a fake account.

I was told by someone who called themselves a "twin flame guru" that I was cursed. She did a ceremony to try and get the negative entity that apparently surrounded me to leave. She said it kept coming back. I paid her over $1500 over the course of six months to try and have this negative entity removed. She said we needed something stronger, and it would cost me an additional $4500. She wanted to place the negative curse that was put on me into an expensive amulet and bury it. I could never see the amulet, and she would take care of everything. That's when I gave my head a shake and realized I was being played.

I have had people reach out saying "I am a spiritualist. I help connect you with your ancestors and do healing spells. All my spells are 100% effective and guaranteed to work." Spells promising my twin flame's return, love, money, fertility, luck, success, protection, healing diseases and so much more.

I had another "healer" inform me that my soul was no longer my soul, and that I had an imposter soul within my body. In order to remove the imposter soul, she wanted to do a ceremony where she would remove that soul and put my soul back in. Then she would realign my chakras. This entire process would cost $2000. I was so desperate. I felt as if I had been cursed as my entire life was falling apart. I actually had the money in my hand to pay her when spirit gave me multiple red flags that this was a scam.

I spoke with someone who was a twin flame coach. She offered a free phone consultation to see if I would be a candidate to be part of her "twin flame program." She went on to tell me that it would cost $6000 to join her program and then an additional $44 a month to be a part of their social media group moving forward. She offered me a payment plan with a guarantee that if I did the program, my twin flame would come into my life once the course had been completed or I would get a full refund. I turned this opportunity down as this was not the right program for me. I wasn't looking to bring my twin flame into my life. I knew who my twin flame was, and I was looking to heal from the connection. I still receive texts and emails about payment plans and black Friday sales.

I was scammed by so many people and wasted so much money. I even had someone reach out who claimed to be with a book marketing company. I looked up the company, and it was a real company. I paid $250 to have them review and promote my book. In turn, I ended up with no legitimate reviews and over three thousand computer-generated fake people on my account who were also trying to scam me by paying for more promotions.

I felt so stupid for falling for it. However, a lot of the time, these scammers looked professional, and it was hard to tell who was real and who was not. The best advice I can give you is if someone reaches out to you, odds are they are trying to take your money and run. Real professionals and healers don't reach out, rather you are guided to them. Use PayPal and not your real credit card number if you are going to pay for online services.

CHAPTER SEVEN

How to Set Boundaries

I used to let people walk all over me. I never stood up for myself. I was one of those people who always said "yes" and didn't know how to say "no." When I started to set boundaries, many friends and family members didn't like the fact that I was now saying "no." They took it as me being selfish and self-centered. Whereas in my reality, I had let them take advantage of me for too long.

I started to set boundaries with friends and family members. Before the awakening, if someone called me out of the blue or needed help with something, I would just drop everything I was doing. I now ask that they give me advanced notice. I refuse to stop what I am doing just to go help someone else.

I started saying "no" to things I didn't want to do. I stopped loaning out money, which shocked a lot of people because they relayed on me to help them out in so many different ways. On occasion, I would ask someone for help with something. I found myself always being the helper. I realized that I was neglecting myself and my needs. *If the roles were reversed, would these people stop everything they were doing to help me? Would they loan me money?*

I made it clear to others that I was going through something and needed time to self-reflect. I needed to spend some time alone. I set my boundaries with those in my life, and if they couldn't respect my boundaries, then I released them from my circle. I lost a lot of "friends" along the way, but those were not real friends to begin with.

I also had to learn to set boundaries with spirit as I was getting constant messages and downloads. It was overwhelming. I didn't know how to make it stop. I could no longer sleep through the night and was feeling constantly tired, drained and depleted. I made it clear that while I was sleeping, I wanted to be left alone and not woken up in the middle of the night. I set the intention that if they had a message for me to place it in a dream. I was open to receiving messages throughout the day. However, I needed a good night's sleep in order to function.

CHAPTER EIGHT

How to Navigate a Spiritual Awakening

***Congratulations, you experienced an awakening!
Now what?***

A spiritual awakening can be very scary if you don't know what's happening. An awakening can be triggered by many different factors. For example: a near-death experience, trauma, a soul connection, hallucinogens, and even the Covid pandemic/lockdowns can be the catalyst for many to wake up.

You may not have experienced the kundalini fireball like I did, and I hope for your sake you didn't. I have now been informed that the way that the kundalini activated within me could have killed me. I have had many near-death experiences in this lifetime, and each time I became more aware and in tune with spirit. It wasn't until the kundalini activation that everything went haywire.

I have had people ask me how to activate the kundalini within to experience what I did.

Why would anyone want to activate the kundalini like that? I thought I was going to die!

It was overwhelming, scary, and my entire life as I knew it fell apart within four months' time.

After the kundalini woke within me, I thought I was going insane. I couldn't eat. I would throw up. I was struggling to sleep through the night. I could hear my own thoughts, spirit, plus my twin flame in my head. I was seeing shadows and orbs. Things were going crazy. Lights would flicker around me, electronics wouldn't work properly, spoons were flying off tables, the paint supply cart at work rolled across the room, I spoke to a dead person on the phone not knowing they were dead, lots of weird things were happening. The worst part was no one believed me.

My entire life as I knew it fell apart within such a short period of time. Anything you're thinking about cutting out of your life will just automatically fall away when you experience an awakening. I left my husband, cat, all my things and house. I lost my job shortly after that and wasn't sure how I was going to survive financially.

I wanted to move out into nature and live off the land. I had no desire for materialistic things. I lost my sense of purpose. The life that I was living was no longer fueling my soul. I went through an "ego death" and something called "the dark night of the soul," which was one of the darkest periods in my life during which I couldn't see the light at the end of the tunnel. I spent a lot of time alone, isolated, crying, not knowing who I could turn to. I started reprocessing all of my trauma on a soul level not only from this lifetime but previous ones. As everything began to surface at an alarming rate, I didn't know how to reprocess it all. To top it off, everyone I spoke to about what was happening to me just kept confirming that I was crazy.

People who I thought were friends walked out of my life. I eliminated those who I found to be toxic. I couldn't stand to be around certain people due to the fact that their energy was making me feel physically sick.

If you're trying to activate the kundalini, I do suggest that you practice these things below as it will come in handy when you do go through an awakening.

Important tips for an awakening:

Ground yourself multiple times a day
Meditate
Eat healthy (your body will start to reject certain foods)
Exercise
Connect with nature
Set boundaries
Stop drinking alcohol or taking any other drugs/ substances that can alter your perception
Work on self-love, self-worth, self-confidence, self-care, self-healing, self-awareness, self-respect
Protect your energy
Connect with your guides
Trust your intuition, write things down
Breathing techniques

FYI: If you are already curious about an awakening, interested in mediation, yoga, crystals, tarot, spirit, seeing angel numbers, surrounding yourself with nature and are already open to the idea of an awakening, you are already awakening. Everyone awakens differently. There might not be the bells and whistles. It might be slow, gradual and develop over time.

Warning! When it comes to drinking alcohol or partaking in any drugs, know that you are now an awakened soul within a body. You need to be grounded in your body at all times, as other spirits can now use your human body as a vessel. For example, if you were to get blackout drunk and not remember what happened the night before, it might feel as if you weren't even there because you don't remember what happened. Odds are you weren't there, and something else had control of your body. Drugs and alcohol also lower your energetic vibration and can bring you down to a depressed state. These things are used to mask the root problems and make you feel numb. When used in access, they can be very dangerous while going through an awakening. I became so physically ill that now I can't even have a glass of wine without throwing up and feeling as if I am having an out-of-body experience.

I had an experience when I was sixteen years old. I was playing with a Ouija board. I had a couple drinks and was just playing with what I thought was a "game." The planchette began to move in a figure 8 motion. It began to move quicker as I sat there mesmerized by the fact that this thing was moving on its own. I felt a hot flash moving through my entire body from my feet up to my head. My body became heavy, that same feeling you get when your foot falls asleep with pins and needles. This feeling crept up from my feet right out the top of my head. I blacked out and woke up the next day blocks away from my house under a tree. I had no clue what happened, or how I got there. No one who was at the house that night would talk to me about it, nor did they speak to me again.

Take caution if you are going to attempt any out-of-body experience as this seems to be a popular thing right now. I hear a lot of people who are woke speaking about partaking in things like psychedelic mushrooms, peyote or ayahuasca. Although these things are "natural," know that any hallucinogen should only be done under the supervision of someone who knows how to bring you back if something goes wrong. These experiences are real, and you could die the first time you try it. Not everything in this world is love and light.

After my awakening, I now experience what is called ascension symptoms. Think of it as leveling up in a video game called life. I thought I was actually really sick for months. I now know that what I experience are ascension symptoms. Ascension symptoms seem to run with the full moon cycle and once you are awake so to speak it is a never ending process. Just to be sure that you don't have anything medically wrong with you, seek a doctor's professional opinion. I experience ascension symptoms out of the blue with no warning. It continues to happen on a regular basis, and I am well aware of what is happening.

Ascension symptoms:

- *Headaches*
- *Sweating*
- *Blurred vision*
- *Body aches/pins and needles*
- *Ringing in the ears*
- *Chills/cold hands and feet*
- *Heart fluttering*
- *Hand skin peeling/sparkly palms*
- *Thirsty*
- *Nausea/vomiting without warning*
- *Vivid dreams*
- *Flu-like symptoms*
- *Astral travel*
- *Floaty feeling*
- *Anxiety*
- *Dizzy spells*
- *Depression*
- *Shortness of breath*
- *Loss of appetite*
- *Food intolerances*
- *Coughing*
- *Diarrhea*
- *Eye twitches*
- *Feeling tired/exhausted all the time*
- *Seeing energy spots*
- *Seeing shadows/orbs*
- *Feeling energy*
- *Not feeling like yourself*
- *Weight loss*
- *Weight Gain*

Don't worry, I went to see my family doctor. She did lots of medical testing. She came to the conclusion that nothing was medically wrong with me. My ascension symptoms run on a full moon cycle. It is definitely more intense during the full moon. Things like the Lion's Gate Portal and eclipses really intensify my symptoms.

I am not going to sugar coat it. A spiritual awakening is by far the scariest, life shattering experience, that I have ever had to navigate myself through. It's a never ending rollercoaster ride of emotions. Some days are good, where I feel as if I can accomplish anything. Some days are bad, where I want to crawl into bed and die. Just when I think I'm on the right path and feeling on top of the world, something triggers more shadows and reflects back something else that's still unhealed. No person will ever be healed to one-hundred percent, because healing isn't linear. Healing is a never ending process and no one is perfect. *Even healers need healers.*

It's one thing to go through a spiritual awakening under normal circumstances. It's a whole new ball game trying to navigate your way through the darkness when you add a pandemic to the mix. I needed to take time to myself. Away from work, home, people, main stream media and society. I took time to do a lot of self-reflection to discover what I want out of life. I also took time to grieve the loss of the life I once had, the person I once was, and the world I once knew.

Have you taken the time to grieve?

CHAPTER NINE

How to Trust Your Intuition

Your intuition is that inner knowing. It's that feeling that you don't know how you know, but you just know. It's also that gut feeling you get when something is wrong. It's that feeling of nauseous butterflies in your stomach. For me, the messages are starting to get easier to read. My ears will start to ring, and I will get a vision of what is going on. I also get angel numbers, messages in song lyrics, memes and signs from the beyond. I am so grateful for this gift, although at times it can feel like a curse.

Connecting with angels and spirit guides

First of all, ask them when you need guidance or protection. Call upon an angel for help (for example,

Archangel Michael) or your own personal spirit guide. We all have angels protecting us. I also have Mabel, my spirit guide. I ask for answers in my dreams. I will state the intention if I am looking for a specific answer to a question. I ask to remember the answer when I wake up. If it doesn't happen right away, it might take a few tries as sometimes the answers are hidden in symbols within dreams. I keep a dream journal next to my bed to write down my thoughts when they come to me.

I also receive messages in my waking life. I pay attention to song lyrics, spirit sends me a lot of messages through song. I also see repeating numbers such as 11:11, 1:11, 2:22, 3:33, 4:44, 5:55, 12:12, 12:34, and the list goes on and on. I pay attention to what I am dong at these times when I glance at the clock or if I am woken up suddenly by spirit. For the longest time, my alarm clock would go off at 12:34 a.m. every morning even when I didn't have it set to go off. I also google search the angel numbers when I see them.

I play the game hot or cold. If I am looking for an object I will ask spirit for guidance finding it, for example my car keys. I will look in a direction and in my head I will intuitively know if I'm hot or cold. I go more in-depth how I used this method in my first book.

I use oracle decks, tarot cards, and a pendulum to clarify messages. I will also put the pen in my non-dominant hand and write messages as they come in. I write yes/no on a paper and hold the pen in my non-dominant hand, hovering over the paper, and it will point to the answer.

I became addicted to tarot card readings when I first made contact with my twin flame. I wanted to know everything:

> *What was happening?*
> *What should I do?*
> *What was he experiencing?*
> *Why was he ghosting me?*
> *What was blocking him from speaking to me?*
> *Would he come back? And if so, when?*

I would pay for a different reading once or twice a week from multiple readers. The problem with tarot card readings on a twin flame is you are one soul and one energy. So there is no separation. Physical separation is only an illusion, as the soul doesn't know separation. That's why with so many readers, they would tell me that my twin flame was coming back soon. If the person doing the reading was not on the twin flame journey themselves, they wouldn't understand the twin flame connection. The more readings I had done and looked outside myself for answers, the more confused I became.

Multiple readers told me that he felt the connection too. Many verified that we are twin flames (which I already knew we were, so I didn't need someone to verify that). I was told that he would be coming back soon, within the next one to three days, three to five weeks, two to three months, or one to two years. I kept waiting on his return and continued to get readings, only to become more disappointed that the readings were not coming true.

I have now given up on going to tarot card readers. I was letting far too many people into my energy field, plus it was becoming overwhelming. I have surrendered to the connection. The more I let go of the thought of my twin flame ever coming back, the easier it was to carry on with everyday life.

Tarot card readings are okay once and awhile to check in with the current energy within yourself, to see where you are in life, and to ask for spirit's guidance. I just find that so many readers now are playing on the twin flame label, and everyone is in search of their twin flame or soulmate. It's best to stay present in the moment. Live your life as it comes, let go of all expectations, and forget about the twin flame or soulmate label.

You will never miss out on something that is meant to happen in your life once you're living your best life. Only then can you be with who you're supposed to be with, once you know who you are. Have faith and trust that everything will work out in divine time.

I learned to trust my own inner knowing, intuition and higher self. I had done past life regression therapy sessions, and I knew how my past lives were interconnected to my current life and exactly why this was all playing out the way it had. Connecting to my higher self and guides has been life-changing for me. I connect during mediation, dreams, hypnosis, and even during my waking hours I ask for messages. Ask and you shall receive. Angel messages are all around, it's simply whether or not you are open to interpreting what your guides are trying to tell you.

I find random objects in random places that will remind me of someone who has passed. I find dimes everywhere; they even fall out of thin air and get thrown at me. I see feathers in random places. I read road signs and license plates and just laugh when I see the messages. I pay attention to the thought I get when my ears start to ring.

Trusting your intuition

- *Ask questions.*
- *Answer your own questions.*
- *Just write (spirit answers me while I'm writing or typing if I go on auto pilot).*
- *Trust that gut feeling.*
- *Ask spirit guides for guidance (signs, symbols, dreams).*
- *Look up the symbolic meanings of your dreams.*
- *Pull a daily oracle card or ask for a song for answers to your questions.*
- *Use a pendulum (I have videos on my social media pages on how to do this).*
- *The answers to all the questions you want answered lies within you (not someone else).*
- *Learn to trust yourself.*
- *Trust your inner knowing.*

We are all born with spirit guides, and we all have this ability to speak to our higher selves and tap into our own intuition and inner knowing. It's just about remembering how to do that. For me, it was as if I had amnesia, and when I experienced the kundalini awakening, the amnesia went away. I remembered everything from every lifetime I have ever lived. I remembered why I was here. I remembered my purpose, my mission, my life goals, and soul contract. I know exactly why everything had to happen the way that it did to bring me to where I am today.

Messages are everywhere.
We just need to be open to receiving
them in unexpected ways.

CHAPTER TEN

The Power of Thoughts

---

*"One drop of water falling into water will send
a ripple out to the edges of its containment.
But one thought, be it negative or positive, has
the whole universe to ripple through.
So watch your thoughts."*
Daphne Rose Johnson

The more positive vibes you put out, the more positive vibes you will attract back. For example, I have worked with seniors in both the community as well as long-term care. Here is the secret to living a long prosperous life!

I would like to share the story of someone I will call Mr. Smith. Mr. Smith had a stroke in his late seventies, which was life-changing for him. After the stroke, Mr. Smith was in a wheelchair and had lost mobility on one side of his body. He wasn't going to let a stroke bring him down. He went to a stroke rehabilitation program where he was able to build his muscles and regain his mobility. He had also lost some of his speech and worked with a speech pathologist.

By the time Mr. Smith joined my exercise class, he was in his nineties and was in pretty good shape. I was teaching exercise classes for seniors out in the community. My classes would incorporate balance, strength, coordination and stretches. The class could be done sitting down in a chair or standing up. Mr. Smith was determined to maintain his healthy lifestyle. By the time Mr. Smith graduated from my class, he advanced to a gym specifically for seniors over the age of sixty-five.

When I went to follow up to see how he was doing, he could run laps around me, bench press more than I could, and do more chin-ups than me too. I watched how positive he was. He was determined that a stroke wasn't going to stop him. Mr. Smith was able to go home and live his life to the fullest.

The last time I saw him he would have been nearing one-hundred years old. He was planning a trip to Europe with his girlfriend who he was going to propose to while on vacation. Mr. Smith taught me that. You're never too old to make changes to your life. You're only as old as you feel, and age is just a number. I know within his heart and soul that he felt as if he were twenty years old.

Although externally, he was obviously older, he did not look anywhere near one hundred. His girlfriend was in her eighties, and they looked to be the same age. Mr. Smith had such a zest for life. *I strive to live my life like him.*

Now I would like to share another story with you. We will call her Mrs. Jones. I was volunteering in long-term care home as a high school student. Mrs. Jones was only sixty-five years old. Mrs. Jones was diagnosed with osteoporosis. She had a fall and broke a hip, so she was in a wheelchair. I would ask Mrs. Jones if she would like to play cards, bingo, board games, paint, exercise, bake, and so much more. You name it, I offered it, and she would refuse. Mrs. Jones would tell me that I didn't understand how much pain she was in.

Prior to her fall, Mrs. Jones enjoyed going out with her friends. She would also socialize and play cards and other games. She spent a lot of time with her family and would watch her grandchildren while their parents were at work. She did a variety of activities with them. After her fall, Mrs. Jones felt useless. She refused physio rehab and exercise. I would continuously try and motivate her to participate in activities she once enjoyed. She would kindly decline and spent the majority of her time in bed sleeping or watching TV.

Within six months' time, I watched as Mrs. Jones quickly declined. Mrs. Jones' mentality was very negative: *woe is me, my life sucks, go away and leave me alone.* I could tell that she was depressed. Mrs. Jones would tell me daily that she had no quality of life, and that life was no longer worth living, and she might as well be dead. She had made a comment that she was just waiting for the snow to melt before she died. That way, her family wouldn't have to stand out in the cold snow for her funeral. That spring, Mrs. Jones died in her sleep.

It's all about the power of your thoughts!

When it comes to financial abundance, many people stay in a place of lack. For example, you have $10 in the bank. There are two different ways of thinking about this. The positive would be: "I am so grateful that I have money in the bank. I am financially abundant and always will be." The negative would be: "I don't have any money. I'm broke. I can't afford to buy what I want, and I never have enough money to do the things I want to do."

If you always focus on what you're lacking in life, you will always lack. If you focus on what you are grateful for and your abundance, you will always be abundant and have everything your heart desires.

"The rich get richer and the poor get poorer."
Percy Bysshe Shelley

Manifesting your dreams into reality

- Make a list of things you want to accomplish (goals).
- Set the intention of what you want to attract into your life.
- Feel as if it has already happened.
- It's the feeling and the energetic frequency you are putting out to the universe.
- Feel the excitement within, like a kid on Christmas morning.
- Forget about the how it will happen, just release it to the universe.
- Don't put a time frame on the outcome.
- Expect the unexpected. We manifest thing into our life in a serendipitous way.
- Draw pictures, make a vision board, or write a list of things you want to manifest.
- Be grateful for the things you currently have in your life.
- Thank the universe for the little things you start to attract into your life.
- The more you give, the more you will receive.
- Focus on the positive and feel the positive vibration within you.

Everything that I need I already have,
everything that I want is attracted to me!

When your energy works against you

If you are constantly in what I call fear-based energy, fearing something bad is going to happen, then that's what you will attract into your life. Ever notice those people who are always sick, saying things like "Woe is me, my life sucks, why do bad things always happen to me?" I call these people soul suckers.

That is not the energy you're striving to be in. I try to steer clear of these individuals. I don't watch the news or pay attention to all the fear-based energy that is happening in the world. You would be surprised how when you disconnect from mainstream media, your life becomes more "normal."

<u>Ego-based energy</u>

This is the individual who feels as if they are superior to everyone else. They make a showcase over their good deeds, seeking external gratification from others. When we come from a place of ego and seeking praise from the outside world, it takes away from the good deed.

It's best to act out of the kindness of your own heart. Just because you don't post it all over social media or advertise what you have done, doesn't mean it's gone unnoticed.

It's all about how it makes you feel!

At the end of the day, we are all connected as one universal God energy source. We are pure love and light. No one is better than an another; we are all created equal. It doesn't matter what others think about you or how they choose to live their life. You can only live your life for you.

Attracting positive people into your life

Write a list of all the qualities you are looking for in a partnership, friendships, coworkers, and neighbours. I try not to focus so much on physical qualities. I made a list of one hundred qualities I was looking for in a romantic partner. I kissed it with bright red lipstick and signed it. I placed dried up red rose petals inside the envelope. I sealed the envelope, sprayed it with a little perfume, and kissed it again. I set the intention, then put the envelope in my sock drawer and left it.

I am attracting people into my life in unexpected ways. I have men ask me out while waiting in line at a store, while out walking the dog and so many other random places. I shifted my energy to more of a "pick me, I'm single and high vibration," over the "pick on me" vibe that I used to attract into my life.

Not to sound conceited, but who wouldn't want to be with me? I am beautiful inside and out. I know my self-worth. I am loving, caring, kind, compassionate, adventurous, and outdoorsy. I have hopes, goals, and dreams for my future. I have so many great qualities, the list goes on and on. The question now is . . .

Who is worthy of my love?

Navigating the energetic connection in a relationship

Regardless of if you are on the twin flame journey or not, we all have energy that pushes people away from us or draws them closer. There is what I call chaser energy, which I explain about in my first book. It's an energy of needing or wanting something so bad that you actually push it away from you.

It's all about balancing the energy within yourself. What it comes down to is self-love and caring for yourself. That's why I started this book with the 30 Day Self-Love and Care Challenge. These are all the ways I learned to find balance within my life by doing things that I enjoy. These activities are the way to my heart and soul, which in turn lit the flame of unconditional love within me.

When we come from a place of want and neediness, we tend to push the thing we want the most away with our energy. Once the energy is balanced and you're happy living life on your own, loving yourself just the way you are, that's when you will unexpectedly attract your dream life into reality.

Ever notice that even after you leave a toxic situation with someone, you continue to attract that same type of person into your life over and over? You will notice the same personality traits, only they will be within a different physical person. When we jump from one relationship to the next without taking the time to heal and work on our own personal soul growth. We tend to become codependent on someone new to make us happy. This in turn can create a trauma bond with the new person and the cycle repeats. Take the time to heal yourself before jumping into a new relationship.

Take time to heal!

This is the time to break the cycle, raise your vibration, know your worth and don't settle for anything less than what you deserve. Know that you deserve the best. Your perfect match is out there, just be patience and they will be magnetized into your life when you least expect it.

"You can never miss out on what's meant for you."
Brigitte van Tuijl

Chapter Eleven

How to Navigate Your Journey

The most frequently asked questions I get regarding the twin flame journey . . .

How do I know if someone is my twin flame or soulmate?

First of all, if you're asking this question, they are neither. The twin flame connection is very rare. Most who are actually on the twin flame rollercoaster of a lifetime, want off the ride. I go in-depth with the different soul connections in my first book. The most important piece of advice I could give you would be to forget about the labels. Ask yourself . . .

> *Do they love and respect me?*
> *Do they treat me how I deserve to be treated?*
> *Is the love mutual?*
> *Do we have the same hopes and dreams?*
> *Does the label really matter if we're in love?*

I have connected with my twin flame, and I think I'm going crazy. How do I make this obsessive thinking stop?

You make the obsession stop by focusing your energy on you. Participate in activities you enjoy, live life in the moment, be present in every moment, meditate, ground yourself, stop worrying about them and what they're doing. Stop watching tarot card readings. Seek closure energetically within yourself. The purpose of the twin flame journey is to find the love within. Your twin flame is you. Separation is an illusion, and you're always connected as one soul.

I have done the work, so why hasn't my twin flame come back yet?

If you're asking this question, there is still more work to be done. Once you feel peace within and no longer want your twin flame to come back into your life, only then will you have truly surrendered to the connection. Although, in the heat of the moment, I had no clue how I would be able to live my life without my twin flame. I am open to him returning, but I no longer feel empty without him. I know that either way I am okay, with or without him in my life. Even if you do the "work," it doesn't guarantee that your twin flame will return.

> *"If you love someone, set them free.*
> *If they come back, they're yours; if*
> *they don't, they never were."*
> Richard Bach

Questions to ask yourself:

1) *Who am I?*
2) *What is my purpose?*
3) *What is my why?*
4) *What do I want to accomplish in this lifetime?*
5) *How can I make my life better?*
6) *Am I living my best life?*
7) *What does my dream life look like?*
8) *What is stopping me from pursuing my dreams?*
9) *How do I feel?*
10) *What am I afraid of?*

11) *What is holding me back?*

12) *Am I currently seeking approval from others outside of myself?*

13) *How am I connecting to my mind, body and soul?*

14) *What fuels my soul?*

15) *How do I want to be remembered?*

16) *Am I living my life with no regrets?*

17) *Am I taking chances?*

18) *Is everyone in my life here for my highest good?*

19) *Am I fully connected to nature and disconnected from social media?*

20) *Am I living life in the moment?*

21) *How do I reprocess trauma and release stored negative emotions?*

22) *How do I fuel my soul?*

23) *What makes me happy?*

24) *What inspires me?*

25) *Have I 100% forgiven myself and others on an energetic level?*

26) *What have I learned from participating in the activities in this book?*

27) *What more could I be doing to heal myself?*

28) *Do I love and respect myself exactly as I am?*

29) *Do I love me, all of me?*

30) *What other questions can you ask yourself?*

"Question everything!"
Albert Einstein

In conclusion, all the answers I was looking for outside of myself were within me the entire time. I didn't need to know how energy works, the philosophy or the science behind it all. I just needed to learn how to heal MYSELF!

Some of the advice I received was to just forget about the past, focus on the now, block and delete my twin flame out of my life and move on. I no longer expect or wait for him to message me. I will always hold a place for him within my heart and soul. I was able to detach in other ways, to free myself from the twin flame connection. It was obsessive, and I wasn't able to focus on my everyday life. However, if it wasn't obsessive like that, I wouldn't have put in the work to change my life. I knew that in order for me to move forward, I needed to reprocess and heal my past trauma and inner wounds.

I became frustrated when I was doing exactly what these "professionals" were telling me to do, and yet my twin flame never came back. I would walk around wearing a happy face while my entire life fell apart. I missed him so much that it felt like a piece of me was missing. Then I realized how the twin flame connection had been romanticized. When in reality, that person was brought into my life to push me in ways I never knew were possible. The purpose of the connection was for me to heal **MYSELF**!

The 30 Day Self-Love and Care Challenge was the best thing I could have created. Along with learning to live life in the moment and just quieting the mind, grounding myself paired with meditation and visualization techniques were game changers. Here I am over two years later, and I am a completely different person. I am now the professional navigating my own life and guiding others.

Everybody is on their own journey. I can't tell you exactly step by step what to do. Only you know for yourself how to heal within. These are the things that worked for me. What worked for me may not be what heals your soul. My goal is that you've learned something from this guide book. If you are able to take away one new skill, then my job is complete.

"It's not the destination, it's the journey!"
Ralph Waldo Emerson

Please feel free to reach out and contact me
personally if you are still unsure how to proceed.
I am offering 1:1 online coaching!

www.myasoul1111.com

mya.soul.1111@outlook.com
I wish you all the best in navigating
your own journey . . .

About the Author

Mya Soul is a strong, independent woman. After experiencing a lifetime of heartache, pain and trauma, she pulled herself up out of a deep dark place and found the light. Mya experienced a kundalini spiritual awakening after connecting with her twin flame. With the help of spirit, along with other healers and guides, she was able to navigate her way through the dark night of the soul. Mya has an extensive background working in the field of recreation and leisure as well as overall health and wellness. Mya started her career working at the YMCA. She then went on to travel the world, working with children on a cruise ship. Mya continued her career working with seniors in long-term care as well as teaching functional fitness for over twenty years of her life. Mya once again has shifted her career path and is expanding her portfolio.

If you are still unsure how to navigate your journey after reading this book, feel free to reach out to Mya personally as she is now offering personal 1:1 online coaching.

www.myasoul1111.com

9 780228 873150